MOVIN' UP

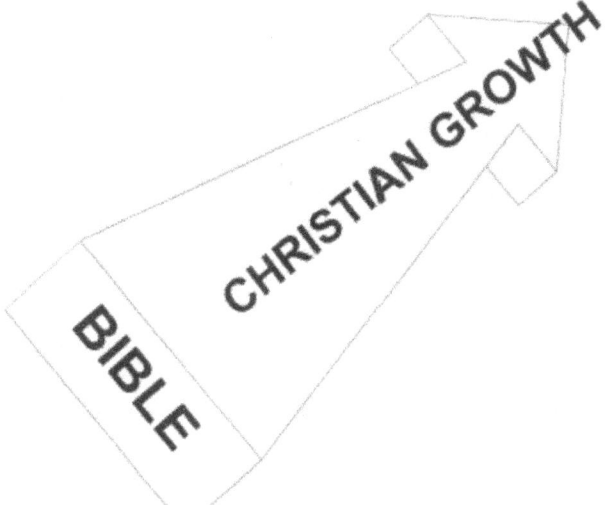

SPIRITUALLY

Encouragement for Christian Maturity

Robert D. Kaiser

ISBN 978-1-63630-429-8 (Paperback)
ISBN 978-1-63630-430-4 (Digital)

Copyright © 2020 Robert D. Kaiser
All rights reserved
First Edition

All rights reserved. No part of this publication may be reproduced, distributed, or transmitted in any form or by any means, including photocopying, recording, or other electronic or mechanical methods without the prior written permission of the publisher. For permission requests, solicit the publisher via the address below.

Covenant Books, Inc.
11661 Hwy 707
Murrells Inlet, SC 29576
www.covenantbooks.com

CONTENTS

Preface 5
Introduction 7

Growin' Up 11
Marryin' Up 25
Raisin' Up 40
Leadin' Up 52
Maturin' Up 66

Summary 73

PREFACE

In sharing the knowledge and wisdom of the Bible that God has provided, we often hear "The Bible is great, but I don't have time to read" or "I don't understand many of the things being said." Why is it that we have time for other things we want to do but don't have time to move up spiritually? And if we don't understand, why not try to find out what it is that we don't understand?

If you want to be a Christian, mature as a Christian, and follow the pathway Jesus has set for you, you need to have a desire for the Word of God.

No matter who you are or what activities you undertake, The Word is important for each one to walk the pathways of life. Christianity is the Christian's way of life, and only through Jesus can a Christian have true life. Jesus said in John 14:6, "I am the way and the truth and the life." It is with this recognition that we must want to know more about Jesus, The Word.

Your growth in the Word will give you greater insight in how to work with people, how to understand yourself, and above all, how to love others as God loves you.

INTRODUCTION

We all seem to be looking to be movin' up in many ways. We hope or expect to move up in our jobs, in housing, in relationships, with vehicles, and in many other ways. If this is so, then why is it that we don't seem as interested in moving up spiritually?

Therefore, this text is put together to assist you in moving upward in your spiritual growth. As we study through the Word, we find that the true teacher is the Word and the Holy Spirit, who will lead us into all truth. This text is nothing more than a guide to try to point you to the Word and the Holy Spirit. As Christians, we should remember Acts 2:38—"Repent and be baptized, every one of you, in the name of Jesus Christ for the forgiveness of sin. And you will receive the gift of the Holy Spirit."

Knowing that if we've repented and been buried with Christ for the forgiveness of our sins, we have the Holy Spirit within, then let's look at the Gospel of John.

> If you love me, you will obey what I command. And I will ask the Father, and he will give you another Counselor to be with you *forever*—the Spirit of truth. The world cannot accept him, because it neither sees him nor knows him. But you know him, for *he lives with you* and *will be in you*. (John 14:15–17, emphasis added)

Notice that in this scripture, it says the Spirit of truth will be with you forever, and "he lives with you and will be in you."

> All this I have spoken while still with you. But the Counselor, the Holy Spirit, whom the Father

will send in my name, *will teach you all things* and will remind you of everything I have said to you. (John 14:25–26, emphases added)

The Holy Spirit is the one whom the Father sends to us, and He will teach us all things. We have to be ready and willing to receive what He has to provide. Often we are unprepared to learn and therefore miss what is being provided. This is similar to children who are in school, yet they are not prepared for their lessons or are unwilling to listen or pay attention. Christians so often pattern themselves after schoolchildren and sometimes try to apply the same logic to their spiritual growth. One thing you cannot do is move up if you cannot be trained to learn.

When we became Christians, as the scriptures say, we are babes in Christ, yet there is so much to learn, but we aren't ready yet. That's like taking your preschooler and teaching calculus or physics before they learn the basics. Christians are the same way. We need to be grounded in the basics of what we believe before we can know to put it into practice. Many times, we put the cart before the horse and head off with a loud charge. But where are we headed? Jesus points this out to us.

I have much more to say to you, *more than you can now bear*. But when he, the Spirit of truth, comes, he will *guide you into all truth*. He will not speak on his own; he will speak only what he hears, and he will tell you what is yet to come. (John 16:12–13, emphasis added)

It is important that we recognize the value of the spirit within and what He can do for us if we let Him. Many times, we will walk the pathways of life and run into problems or situations that we try to handle ourselves.

It is important, therefore, to recognize that in 1 Corinthians 2:6, it says, "We do, however, speak a message of wisdom among the mature, but not the *wisdom of this age or of the rulers of this age*, who are coming to nothing" (emphasis added). This passage goes on to reflect that they are talking about Jesus but that God has revealed him to us, and if we KNOW Jesus, then we'll bring Him into our situations. In this chapter of Corinthians, it further states in verses 12 and 13 that "We have not received the spirit of the world but the Spirit who is from God, that *we may understand what God has freely given us*. This is what we speak, not in words taught us by human wisdom but in words taught by the Spirit, expressing spiritual truths in spiritual words" (emphasis added).

One way then to learn is to know the Word, the Bible, or as I like to talk about, the Manufacturer's Handbook. You do this through daily Bible reading, individual study, Bible studies with others, and Bible school programs. We need to do this:

> Do your best to present yourself to God as one approved, a workman who does not need to be ashamed and who correctly *handles* the word of truth. (2 Timothy 2:15, emphasis added)

Prayer is another key element in our spiritual growth. We can see from James 5:16b that "prayer of a righteous man is powerful and effective."

> Elijah was a man just like us. He prayed earnestly that it would not rain, and it did not rain on the land for three and a half years.
> Again he prayed, and the heavens gave rain, and the earth produced its crops. (James 5:17–18)

As Christians, we have confessed Christ, repented of our sins, and have been clothed with Christ through our baptism for the forgiveness of sin and received the gift of the Holy Spirit. Since we have been clothed with Christ through baptism, we have also gone through his death, burial, and resurrection.

> Or don't you know that all of us who were baptized into Christ Jesus were baptized into

> his death? We were therefore buried with him through baptism into death in order that, just as Christ was raised from the dead through the glory of the Father, we too may live a new life. If we have been united with him like this in his death, we will certainly also be united with him in his resurrection. For we know that our old self was crucified with him so that the body of sin might be done away with, that we should no longer be slaves to sin—because anyone who has died has been freed from sin. Now if we died with Christ, we believe that we will also live with him. For we know that since Christ was raised from the dead, he cannot die again; death no longer has mastery over him. The death he died, he died to sin once for all; but the life he lives, he lives to God. In the same way, count yourselves dead to sin but alive to God in Christ Jesus. (Romans 6:3–11)

What a joy it should be for us to know that Christ is around us and in us. We should also recognize that if Christ is in us, then as it states in 1 Corinthians 2:16, "But we have the mind of Christ." This statement can boggle the senses to realize that we could think the way Christ thinks, and we could act the way Christ acts. I believe that if we fully recognize that Christ is here in our lives daily, then we can start to make a difference with our opportunities for moving up in life.

With these things in mind, we will look at some aspects of our lives and see if we can determine how we can get promoted, why are we lagging behind, what should we be doing, with whom we should be working, where we should be going, and when should we be doing these things.

GROWIN' UP

As adults, we are so concerned about our children growing up (physically) that we even go so far as to say at times "Won't you ever grow up." Even young people seem to be occupied with growing older so I can be this and that. Young people want to look older (sophisticated), and growing up seems to occupy our minds. Likewise, adults are very interested in how their children learn. My children must go to the right school district or have teacher so and so. I know parents who have actually moved to insure their children were in the right school district. Why is it then that when it comes to spiritual growth, there is so much laxness about wanting to grow up?

I believe Jesus is interested in our physical growth, and I know He's interested in our spiritual growth. In what is referred to as the Great Commission (Matthew 28:19–20), Jesus says in verse 20, "and teaching them to obey everything I have commanded you." If Jesus believes that there is a need for Christians to grow up, then why aren't we concerned about our families being involved in the right school district, the place where we know they will gain the best spiritual growth? We need to join our forces with the body of Christ and the Holy Spirit and move off the dime and move up, or as God might like to say to us, "Won't you ever grow up?"

This section will talk about growing up spiritually and what we need to look at to figure out how we can continue to move up.

What better way for us to start growing than to know the Bible. What do you know about the Word? The Bible is referred to as the Word of God.

> What two major divisions of the Bible do we have?
> Old Testament and New Testament

How many books in the Bible?
Old Testament: 39 (3 and 9 = 39)
New Testament: 27 (3 x 9 = 27)
Total Books: 66

The Old Testament is divided into how many groups? 5 What are they?
Law (5); History (12); Devotions (5);
Major Prophets (5)
Minor Prophets (12)

The New Testament is divided into how many groups? (5) What are they?
Gospels (4), History (1), Special Letters (14),
General Letters (7), Prophecy (1)

Who does the Bible refer to throughout?
Jesus

These items are things about the Bible that hopefully we learned early as a Christian. Now as we grow with the Lord and really get to know the Word of God, we will start to see the Bible like a mirror to the soul so we can examine ourselves at all times in the light of His teachings. In other words, when I get ready to respond to my spouse in an unnerving situation, what would Jesus do? In my business dealings, what does the Bible teach about dealing with others? If we stop and reflect upon questions such as these, we will get a real chance to see ourselves in the light of the Word.

For each of us to be able to reflect on the Word, we need to spend more time with the Word. I remember a message in a church paper in 1988 by Merv Johnson that goes like this:

> "Words are funny critters. Have you noticed how words are known by the company they keep? For instance, take a common word like 'bright' and notice how it changes with the word it pals

around with such as: sun, or thought, or half. Take the word 'money' and look what other words like much, little, funny, grabber, etc. do to it. So it is with people. We too are shaped and known by the company we keep. As the old farmer said, 'Well, it looks like a hog, and it acts like a hog, and it smells like a hog, and it runs with hogs, so I reckon it must be a hog. The point of all this is that to be a good word among all the griping and blasphemous words of our day, we need to keep company with THE WORD. No association changes us as much as Word association and the more time we spend in IT, the more like Him we become."

This story illustrates that we need to constantly read the Bible, be active in Bible studies, and associate ourselves with the Word in personal study.

Another essential ingredient in our spiritual lives is prayer. There are many passages in the Bible that show Jesus to have need to be in prayer and to have communion with His Father. Why should we be different? Jesus prayed at His baptism (Luke 3:21). At the choosing of the twelve, He spent the night in prayer (Luke 6:12–13). He also prayed after feeding the five thousand (Matthew 14:13–33), prayed for His disciples and the glorification of the church (John 17), and prayed just before His arrest (Matthew 26:36–44). If Jesus was in prayer and His early church was in prayer (Acts), then it seems to reason that we as individuals and as a church body need to be in prayer. We need to be communicating with God.

There are numerous scripture passages about prayer. Here are a few to refresh ourselves.

Each one of us must pray lest we might enter into temptation (Matthew 26:41), confess our sins to God (1 John 1:9), and continually be in prayer (1 Thessalonians 5:17). God hears our prayers (James 5:13–18; Matthew 21:22). As sinners, we are unworthy to stand in the presence of God, but through Jesus, we have access

(Hebrews 4:14–16, 7:24–28, 9:24–26). We must also think of what ingredients we need to have an effective prayer life. I'm sure you can come up with some, but let me share a few with you.

When we come to God in prayer, we must come in humbleness (Luke 18:9–14, Matthew 6:12). Our prayer should not be a parade for the public, but our prayer should come from the depths of our heart with all sincerity. We should not be trying to impress man but to communicate our heartfelt desires and praises to the Father. We must also be forgiven to be effective in communicating with our God. Our Father will not forgive us unless we have forgiven those who have wronged us (Matthew 6:14–15, Mark 11:24–25). I also believe that faith is very essential in our prayer life. We must believe to whom we are speaking, and we must believe that He is capable of handling the situation that we bring before Him. Notice that I refrained from using the words "He answered our prayer." This was done so that we may recognize that God is capable of handling any situation, but not always the way we want Him to handle it. He does answer our prayer about the situation because God loves His children, and He knows what we need to direct the course of our life (Matthew 17:20–21, Mark 11:24, James 5:15–16). The Holy Spirit must be active in our lives. How can the Holy Spirit help us in our lives if we suppress Him and not allow Him to be walking with us daily? In 1 Thessalonians 5:19, it states, "Do not put out the Spirits fire." I like some of the other translations' words for this passage, which states, "Do not stifle the Spirit" (Modern Language); "Do not quench the Spirit" (Revised Standard); "Do not smother the Holy Spirit" (Living Bible). In other words, let the Spirit have full rein in your life and He can be effective.

> In the same way, the Spirit helps us in our weakness. We do not know what we ought to pray for, but the Spirit himself intercedes for us with groans that words cannot express. And he who searches our hearts knows the mind of the Spirit, because the Spirit intercedes for the saints in accordance with God's will. (Romans 8:26–27)

MOVIN' UP SPIRITUALLY

The last item I have in my list is concentration. When we pray, we must concentrate. We need to focus our attention on talking with God and not just to Him. Prayer is a two-way communication with God. It is a time when we have a relationship.

This relationship is to help us adjust to God and not God to us. This doesn't mean that we cannot or should not pray when we cannot give full concentration, such as when we are driving down the road, but it does mean that we should have a desire to communicate with our God, and the concentration comes from our heart.

I believe that Christians sometimes assume the myth that spiritual growth is optional. For instance, I accepted Jesus as my Savior, so I'm okay. I know that a lot of Christians take this attitude either consciously or unconsciously because so many start allowing things of the world to get in the way. It becomes easy to do other things that seem to be more important than to read the Bible, pray, attend services, or study the Bible.

What are some of these worldly things? Let's consider them. There's work, household activities, family outings, SPORTS, and weather, just to name a few. But what does The Word have to say about growing spiritually or moving up?

> Brothers, I could not address you as spiritual but as worldly—mere infants in Christ. I gave you milk, not solid food, for you were not yet ready for it. Indeed, you are still not ready. You are still worldly. For since there is jealousy and quarreling among you, are you not worldly? Are you not acting like mere men? (1 Corinthians 3:1–3)

> I pray that out of his glorious riches he may strengthen you with power through his Spirit in your inner being, so that Christ may dwell in your hearts through faith. And I pray that you, being rooted and established in love, may have power, together with all the saints, to grasp how wide and long and high and deep is the love of Christ,

and to know this love that surpasses knowledge—that you may be filled to the measure of all the fullness of God. (Ephesians 3:16–19)

It was he who gave some to be apostles, some to be prophets, some to be evangelists, and some to be pastors and teaches, to prepare God's people for works of service, so that the body of Christ may be built up until *we all* reach unity in the faith and in the knowledge of the Son of God and become *mature*, attaining to the whole measure of the fullness of Christ. Then we will no longer be infants, tossed back and forth by the waves, and blown here and there by every wind of teaching and by the cunning and craftiness of men in their deceitful scheming. Instead, speaking the truth in love, we will in all things *grow up* into him who is the Head, that is, Christ. From him the whole body, joined and held together by every supporting ligament, grows and builds itself up in love, as each part does its work. (Ephesians 4:11–16, emphasis added)

Be imitators of God, therefore, as dearly loved children and live a life of love, just as Christ loved us and gave himself up for us as a fragrant offering and sacrifice to God. (Ephesians 5:1–2)

We have much to say about this, but it is hard to explain because you are slow to learn. In fact, though by this time you ought to be teachers, you need someone to teach you the elementary truths of God's word all over again. You need milk, not solid food! Anyone who lives on milk, being still an infant, is not acquainted with the teaching about righteousness. But solid food is for the

> *mature*, who by constant use have trained themselves to distinguish good from evil. Therefore let us leave the elementary teachings about Christ and *go on to maturity*, not laying again the foundation of repentance from acts that lead to death, and of faith in God, instruction about baptisms, the laying on of hands, the resurrection of the dead, and eternal judgement. And God permitting, we will do so. (Hebrews 5:11–6:3, emphasis added).

> Like newborn babies, crave pure spiritual milk, so that by it you may *grow up* in your salvation. (1 Peter 2:2, emphasis added)

It would seem that the myth has been wiped out. The Word, I believe, is clear—spiritual growth is not optional. God's Word says it over and over that we must move up and we must grow up. Like it says in Hebrews 5:14, the solid food is for the mature whose faculties have been trained by practice to distinguish between good and evil. You might consider this like an on-the-job training. When sports teams are formed, they don't just play their games. They spend enormous amounts of time in practice (scrimmages) to become proficient at what they do. Look at the professional football teams. They become a moving machine because the players have practiced until they KNOW what they are to do and what they are looking for during plays. Christians need to KNOW the Word and practice the commands of the Word in order for each Christian to KNOW what they are to do and what they need to look for during their life's activities. As an example, let's look at an excerpt from a devotion presented by Reggie White in *Men's Devotional Bible*.

> "How do I handle these threats to my faith? The same way I do as a football player.
> The first step is training. I must study God's Word on a daily basis. Paul wrote to Timothy:

'Do your best to present yourself to God as one approved, a workman who does not need to be ashamed and who correctly handles the word of truth' (2 Timothy 2:15)...

The second focus is on my surroundings. I must also be careful not to surround myself too closely with those who don't believe in God's Word. I have many friends who are not Christians and I sure do love them. But we have a different relationship. Unbelievers just don't have as much in common as believers do. They don't have the same goals, morals or social life that believers in Christ have.

It doesn't take too much sense to realize that you become like those with whom you spend the most time. Know your surroundings and *control them; don't let your surroundings control you.*

Finally, practice what you know is right. *Too often we focus on doing what we've always done.* We don't progress, keep in shape, work out daily..."
(Emphasis added)

Let us focus on what has been emphasized in the above meditation. Reggie White states that we must control our surroundings, not let the surroundings control you. We say we can and do control what is happening around us, yet we don't realize that our surroundings slowly creep up on us when we least expect it. An example I like to use is the way my son drives. He was taught to drive in a small community and how to start smoothly and drive within speed limits and stop smoothly. This he did very precisely; that is, until he moved to a major metropolitan area where traffic was different. People started fast and drove hard and fast and made quick stops. It wasn't long until I noticed that my son had adopted some of the same driving habits that he observed and was surrounded by in the city. I also recall when I moved south that it wasn't long before I picked up the southern accent and some of the terminology that they used. This shows that our surroundings and who we associate with regularly can have a significant impact on our being able to move up. The second point I'd like to emphasize from Mr. White's meditation is that we too often focus on what we've always done. Isn't it amazing how we are creatures of habit? If it's been good for the last thirty years, it must be good for the next. If business carried that attitude, we'd still be adding and subtracting with our fingers or sewing our clothes by hand. However, business and industry said we must progress and we must grow. Christians need to do the same. We need to shake the way we've always done it (tradition) and recognize that we need to make progress. It is our responsibility to work out daily in the Lord and to keep in shape for Him so that we are prepared to serve Him, to honor Him, and to bring honor and glory to Him who is our Lord and Savior. If we can keep in shape, then we will be ready when we go to the next meeting at work to discuss things as Christ would discuss. We will be in position to handle the situation that develops with our friend or neighbor. As Christians, we must understand that Christianity is our way of living. It is not static or immobile but active and progressive. We should not think of ourselves as having reached a plateau, but as Paul states in Philippians 3:8–12, we follow after Christ so that we can attain greater things. Let us not be content with what we have done, but let's move on to the things that are ahead. Moving on to things ahead will enable each one to move up in life. It is time to adjust our lives to God, then He can accomplish His purposes. God has made it possible to attain the very character we need to do all these things (2 Peter 1:1–15). If we build these attributes in our lives, we will grow in character. Our adjustments must put us in the position to obey. In other words, you cannot continue life as usual or stay where you are and go with God at the same time.

Look with me at what you may do at work. Do you have to adjust your life to be in position to obey? It is assumed that on taking your position, you have a supervisor who requires you to be at a given place at a certain time. Does not your employer require that you put in so much time or effort on the job? With this in mind, what would happen if you continued your life as it was before you got this job?

I know if coming out of college was the way it were, then I'd get up late, go to class if I felt like it, wear whatever clothes I wanted, and went home whenever I was ready. If I did that on my first job, chances are, I wouldn't be employed long. No, if I wanted to keep my job and move up in the organization, I needed to fix some things in order to go along with my company.

I firmly believe that many Christians take this position when it comes to growing in Christ. We tend to live our life as usual or are content to stay where we are, and we miss out on going with God.

It appears that we do this because our greatest difficulty in following God comes at the point of adjustment. That's right, adjustment. We must adjust our lives to walk the walk and talk the talk, meaning that our point of view must be like His, and our ways must be like His. What we say and what we do must reflect Jesus Christ. We cannot just talk about Him and not act like Him. Otherwise, we would not be obedient to Him and would dishonor Him. A Christian's life is like a race. Paul described it this way:

> Do you not know that in a race all the runners run, but only one gets the prize? Run in such a way as to get the prize. Everyone who competes in the games goes into strict training. They do it to get a crown that will not last; but we do it to get a crown that will last forever. Therefore I do not run like a man running aimlessly; I do not fight like a man beating the air. No, I beat my body and make it my slave so that after I have preached to others, I myself will not be disqualified for the prize. (1 Corinthians 9:24–27)

If we are to be compared to an athlete, then like an athlete, we must exercise self-control (1 Corinthians 8:25). Self-control involves waiting (patience). Have you ever had to wait on someone, and you waited and waited and waited? It does try your patience, doesn't it? But stop and think about what it may mean. When we are waiting on someone, we have, in a sense, become dependent on them. We are depending on them to come or do what they said so that we can do something. Similarly, waiting on God develops in us an absolute dependence on Him. He says He'll do something, and we depend on it being done. Self-control is not something we assume in times of emergency but is something we have to cultivate and build into our lives (2 Peter 1:5–9). Likewise, an athlete is obedient to instructions. Christians must also do what is commanded by God. His commands are not given so we can pick and choose. It's not like a buffet that you can say "I like this one, so I'll get it, but that one I have a distaste for, and so I'll just let that one go by." No. God expects total obedience out of our loving relationship with Him. Although we may not like it and may not want to do it, the best thing about obedience to God is that His will is always right.

In our race of life, there is a goal to be attained. Paul had his goal in view as he expressed it in Philippians 3:14–16. Abraham and Moses also had theirs. Our goal should likewise be the same goal that has a reward that is beyond expression.

> However, as it is written; 'No eye has seen, no ear has heard, no mind has conceived what God has prepared for those who love him'—but God has revealed it to us by his Spirit… (1 Corinthians 2:9–10)

Our race must be run with patience, endurance, and obedience, for our life must be focused on God and His purpose. As Christians, we need to submit ourselves to Him and let Him show us what to do, or we need to join what we see Him doing around us. Christians must recognize that God is not our servant to do our bidding or satisfy our every want. He is not there to carry out our plans. God desires that we make our lives available to Him and let Him use us as we are His servants, His instruments, and we should serve Him according to His plan, not ours. However, God will allow us to follow our own plans, and He will always be there to help us see the right directions. He would, however, like for us to join Him.

God would like very much for us to get to work where He is working. He would be overjoyed if you would get involved with your congregation. He would love it if you are active in your neighborhood. But you may ask, how do I know where He's working? Let's look at some ways.

Prayer

We've talked about prayer before, and we know it's a way to communicate with God. We can look to God for Him to show us where He is working.

Questions

Once we've prayed, we can ask questions that may open our eyes that something is happening. You might ask someone how you can pray for them, or maybe you perceive that someone needs to talk, so you ask, "Do you want to talk?" Maybe you hear or see someone who is going to do something that requires an additional hand or two, so you ask, "Can I give you a hand?" The right questions will bring out the need, and you can see that God is working.

Listen

There are so many times in life that we miss out on seeing God working because we are not listening. Many times, opportunities abound to share Jesus when we're talking with people, but because we don't listen, we miss the opportunity. Also, if we are listening to people, there are times when they tell you they need help, friendship, love, or maybe a shoulder to cry on. We need to listen to be sensitive to people and not miss out on God working.

Agape Love

The love of God is such that if we display it in our lives, we will not miss out on where he is working. For agape love means we see a need, and we move to meet the need. We don't count the cost of what we have to do, nor do we count the gain. We don't consider worthiness as a factor, and we look at the person's good.

I'm sure there are others we could discuss, but for us to be active and be involved where God is, we must know and recognize that God speaks to us through the Holy Spirit, the Bible, prayer, circumstances, and through His people, the church. I believe that our problem is that we become worldly because we are taught how to organize and plan according to worldly ways, and then we try to carry out our plan. We need to recognize that God wants you and me to follow Him, not a plan. We need to line up what the Bible says with the guidance the Holy Spirit is giving with the circumstances involved, and when they line up, then we can move up.

An old sea captain was talking with another seaman about the difficulties of the harbor and bringing ships to dock. The seaman remarked that the captain always seemed to bring in ships with ease and wanted to know how he did it. The captain told the seaman that he had learned that if he lined up the light from the lighthouse with the light from the church on the hill and the vessel he was in, then it was a straight shot into harbor. We have a similar line up that will guide us in our walk with the Lord. When we get these guides lined up, we need to say "Whatever you want of me, Lord, I will do."

How much involvement does God have in your life? Have you ever stopped to think about the amount of involvement God has in your life? We know God is always working and wants to be involved in everything we do, but we have to let Him.

Let's stop and do a reality check and see what we think God's involvement might be in our activities.

1. When you woke up this morning, did you involve God?
2. When you got dressed, did you involve God?
3. When you ate breakfast, did you involve God?
4. When you talked to your spouse, children, brother, or sister, did you involve God?
5. When you drove to work or other activity, did you involve God?

6. When you interact with coworkers, students, or neighbors, did you involve God?

I believe that many times, we go through our activities and don't think of God or take Him for granted. But if we continuously think about God as we enter into these activities, then God becomes more intimately a part of our thinking, our speech, and our actions. I remember the book *In His Steps* by Sheldon where people made decisions by asking "What would Jesus do?" in each situation in which they were involved. The key if we so involve God in our everyday normal activities, we then become so conscious of God being there that after a while, He will always be in every thought, action, and reaction that we get involved with in our lives. This close association with our Lord is extremely important in our moving up, for we need to recognize and remember that Christianity is our way of life, and "for our struggle is not against flesh and blood but against…the spiritual forces of evil" (Ephesians 6:10–18).

MARRYIN' UP

People who plan to marry have high expectations of happiness. Then after being married, they wonder where all the weeds come from in their own Garden of Eden. A lot of those weeds come from unrealistic expectations of what marriage would do for them. People have said they wished they would have known some of this sooner, but they didn't even know enough to know what they didn't know. It has been reported in research reports that about one-half of all serious marital problems develop in the first two years. However, couples seeking help, on the average, have been married seven years. I believe that if you want it badly enough, a great and wonderful marriage is within your grasp.

Have you ever gone out and purchased some equipment or appliance and bring it home and immediately take it out and try to operate it with just your own intelligence and discover that you're puzzled because it's not doing what you thought? We forgot to read the instructions or owner's manual. Bingo! Now it works much better. We have an owner's manual (Manufacturer's Handbook) that comes with marriage. The Word of God contains that information. As with all manuals, we sometimes need help in understanding the manual. Once again, we learn through our Word association. As I study the Word, I am more impressed with the practical wisdom it provides in every area. Paul wrote this:

> These things happened to them as examples and were written down as warnings for us, on whom the fulfillment of the ages has come. (1 Corinthians 10:11)

I believe the Bible reveals better than any source the secret of a harmonious marriage. There is value in seminars, counselors, and books, but God's Word is as it says in Psalm 119:105: "Your word is a lamb to my feet and a light for my path." Let's start at the beginning to see what God intended in marriage.

> The Lord God said, "It is not good for the man to be alone. I will make a helper suitable for him."
> Now the Lord God had formed out of the ground all the beasts of the field and all the birds of the air.
> He brought them to the man to see what he would name them; and whatever the man called each living creature, that was its name. So the man gave names to all the livestock, the birds of the air and all the beasts of the field.
>
> But for Adam no suitable helper was found. So the Lord God caused the man to fall into a deep sleep; and while he was sleeping, he took one of the man's ribs and closed up the place with flesh. Then the Lord God made a woman from the rib he had taken out of the man, and he brought her to the man.
>
> The man said, "This is now bone of my bones and flesh of my flesh; she shall be called 'woman,' for she was taken out of man." For this reason a man will leave his father and mother and be united to his wife, and they will become one flesh. The man and his wife were both naked, and they felt no shame. (Genesis 2:18–25)

It seems God knew that man does not function well alone, that he needed a helper, a companion. A survey some time ago of men and women showed that the happiest people were most often married men, and the most unhappy persons were unmarried men.

Notice in verse 21 how the woman was formed. God could have made the woman from dust just as He had man and all the animals, yet it is believed that He formed woman from man's rib to show the uniqueness of the close relationship that God designed for man and woman.

An old rabbi story states that God chose a rib from Adam's side, not a bone from Adam's head so that she would be over him, nor a bone from his foot that she would be under him, but from his side that she would be next to him, from under his arm that he might protect her, and from next to his heart that he might love her.

A Christian marriage is to be a positive testimony to the world of Christ's love for the church. God's love is unconditional. It is faithful, and it is sacrificial. So then, when there is a Christian marriage, it is unconditional, faithful, and sacrificial. It's a testimony to the world of how God loves man. So how do we set the stage to have the right marriage? It should start by looking at potential mates before one marries.

Robert Frost in a poem observed that love begins in delight and ends in wisdom. He's not saying that delight comes to a dead end but that love moves up into wisdom.

What is love? Let's look at what the Bible describes as love.

> Love is patient, love is kind. It does not envy, it does not boast, it is not proud. It is not rude, it is not self-seeking, it is not easily angered, it keeps no record of wrongs. Love does not delight in evil but rejoices with the truth. It always protects, always trusts, always hopes, always perseveres. Love never fails. (1 Corinthians 13:4–8a)

So many times, we misunderstand the feeling of love for the real thing. What one needs to build the love of a lifetime happens through treasuring, guarding, and nurturing. We need to recognize that feelings are thoughts of the heart rather than thoughts of the mind.

We recognize that our feelings (emotions) are not capable of conducting our daily affairs, so we don't let them control us. Why do we let them control our love relationships? If we know that feelings do not control our daily affairs, then we need to apply this in our love relationships. Feelings have helped bring couples together, but they aren't designed to drive us anywhere. ONLY GOD'S WORD can guide us in the right direction. We need to remember that feelings are fragile and explosive and need to be handled with care, but you are more than your feelings.

What should we look for in a spouse? The Word gives us some help on this area.

> Do not be yoked together with unbelievers. For what do righteousness and wickedness have in common? Or what fellowship can light have with darkness? What harmony is there between Christ and Belial? What does a believer have in common with an unbeliever? (2 Corinthians 6:14–15)

I also remember a young woman telling me that each time she went out with a young man, she would go home and read 1 Corinthians 13:4–8 in the following manner and asked herself if this is true of the person with whom she went out. Let us assume his name was Don.

> Don is patient, Don is kind. He does not envy, he does not boast, he is not proud. He is not rude, he is not self-seeking, he is not easily angered, he keeps no record of wrongs. Don does not delight in evil but rejoices with the truth. He always protects, always trusts, always hopes, always perseveres. Don never fails.

In using this system, she realizes that men are not perfect, but it gives her a sense of using God's Word as the standard with which to gauge the young men she dates.

Each person has a responsibility to use the Word in determining who would be a good spouse. Each one must learn what the Bible shows is love and not allow infatuation to simulate love, which tends to be for selfish purposes and leads to "trouble in River City."

I also believe it is each parent's responsibility to guide their children in the teachings of the Bible, to assist them in looking at and evaluating in light of the Word each person they date. As parents, we must help them to see what genuine love in a marriage is all about and how that love matures with age by being an example and by discussing love as it's presented in the Scriptures.

For those that are married, hopefully we have been able to see that true (genuine) love makes you long to be together. You just want to be with the other person. You see each other in a unique way, and you see your spouse as extraordinary, priceless, and unique like no one else. You place such high value on each other that you are willing to give up selfish independence, and our attitude toward the other is to drop self and fully desire to serve the other. You also desire to commit yourselves to each other forever.

These things don't just happen overnight, but if we move from falling in love to being in love, to practicing loving your partner (that is, giving and always doing the very best for them), then we will be able to fall in love many times over forever. The love we are talking about is the kind that gives of oneself to another regardless of feelings. It's an act of the will. It's a decision of the mind, a learning to care.

We can learn to love because the Bible commands us to love each other. Multitudes of couples have done it. Look at Isaac and Rebekah in Genesis 24. A wife was gotten for Isaac from his homeland who was willing to relocate. In Genesis 24:67, it says that she became his wife, and then he loved her. He loved her because he made an act of his will, a decision of his mind. Couples can have a foreverness if they (1) make a commitment, (2) pray for God's power, (3) dedicate themselves to fulfilling their mate's needs, and (4) develop spiritual maturity. This last point is extremely important.

> But seek first his kingdom and his righteousness,
> and all these things will be given to you as well.
> (Matthew 6:33)

Individually, we must put God number one. We must desire to grow as Jesus wants us to grow. Our spiritual relationship with God and each other is like a triangle. Note that with God at the top and each of us at the bottom corners, if we as partners grow toward God together, we as a couple will grow closer to one another. And as we grow closer to God, our relationship likewise grows because we come closer together as a couple. The key, however, is both the husband and wife must agree to grow spiritually together.

The benefits of this growth are tremendous. You have a commitment to each other that will be enhanced. You will have Christian friends who will enhance and reinforce your family values. Your ultimate fulfillment is through Jesus, and you become less demanding on your mate. Your spiritual growth together will help you to worship and pray together, an adhesive to the relationship. We need to remember that when Christ is the center of your home, he brings it together. Steven Curtis Chapman has a song titled "I Will Be Here." This song has the following lines:

> "If in the dark we lose sight of love,
> Hold my hand and have no fear
> Because I will be here.
> I will be here and you can cry on my shoulder.
> When the mirror tells us that we are older,
> I will hold you and watch you grow in beauty
> And tell you all the things you are to me,
> And I will be here.
> I will be true to the promise I have made to you
> And to the one who gave."

Our relationship in marriage must be like that. If we looked at Adam and Eve's relationship, we would see that it is exclusive. There was no competition, no comparison, and no other offer. I sometimes wonder if we don't look at marriage like we do when we shop. We look for the competition, and we want to do some comparison shopping. After all, there could be a better offer. Having worked for the government for years, I can assure you that the best offer is not always what it may appear. As marriage partners, we need to realize that our relationship, if developed in the Lord, is to be exclusive. Let's not wonder about that basketball captain or the cheerleader. Let's not complain that he is not as romantic as someone on the TV. We can see that Adam and Eve were committed exclusively to each other. Our marriages should be the same. Our marriages should be based on the thought that this is the person God has provided for me, and I'm going to be the best companion I can be to this one exclusively. I'm giving myself to you and you only till death do us part.

> "Haven't you read," he replied, "that at the beginning the Creator made them male and female, and said 'For this reason a man will leave his father and mother and be united to is wife, and the two will become one flesh?' So they are no longer two, but one. Therefore what God has joined together, let man not separate." (Matthew 19:4–6)

Now let's look at ourselves. Men and women are equally important to God, but they are not created the same. Men and women differ physically, and they differ emotionally. Studies of unborn babies show that the female develops the left side of the brain faster, which has the verbal skills, and males develop the right side of the brain faster, which has the visual and spatial abilities. I am told that the average man speaks approximately twenty-five thousand words a day, and the average woman speaks approximately fifty thousand words a day. Women are loyal to one TV program, while men are channel surfers.

Few people enter a new job without any idea of what they are expected to do, like a job description, yet many people take on marriage and have no idea of what role they are to play. As Christians, we must submit to the Lordship of Jesus, and the Bible (Manufacturer's Handbook) must be the authority in our lives.

Let's begin by looking at the man's role. The first responsibility a man has in marriage is to be the spiritual leader of the home.

> For the husband is the head of the wife as Christ is the head of the church, his body, of which he is the Savior. Now as the church submits to Christ., so also wives should submit to their husbands in everything. (Ephesians 5:23–24)

I believe that God has made it clear what He has designed. God knew that for a happy relationship to exist, there had to be a lead. God created both man and woman and knows the makeup of each one. Abraham was a Christlike leader. He had uncertainty in his life.

Take the time Abraham was to move. He had to make this decision by faith. Now it doesn't say, but I would guess that as a Christlike leader, Abraham had input from Sarah on the situation. However, the Bible does not say that God said to Sarah or that God said to Abraham and Sarah. It says that God said to Abraham "I want you to move" because God had delegated Abraham to be the leader of the home.

> Husbands, love your wives, just as Christ loved the church and gave himself up for her to make her holy, cleansing her by the washing with water through the word, and to present her to himself as a radiant church, without stain or wrinkle or any other blemish, but holy and blameless. In this same way, husbands ought to love their wives as their own bodies. He who loves his wife loves himself. After all, no one ever hated his own body, but he feeds and cares for it, just as Christ

> does the church—for we are members of his body. 'For this reason a man will leave his father and mother and be united to his wife, and the two will become one flesh.' This is a profound mystery—but I am talking about Christ and the church. However, each one of you also must love his wife as he loves himself, and the wife must respect her husband. (Ephesians 5:25–33)

Men, we have to be involved. As a husband God, has given us a responsibility to set the example for involvement and to demonstrate compassion, integrity, temperance, ambition, and spirituality. It is the husband's responsibility to take the initiative, help deal with our children, plan activities, handle finances, attend church and Bible studies, and develop skills in our home.

I remember an elder telling me many years ago that he believed the Bible points out that all activities (all work) is man's and that God made woman as the helpmate for companionship and assistance. He said that when man recognizes that all work activities are his responsibility and woman assists in the team effort that God has provided, the marriage relationship will become more successful.

> Husbands, in the same way be considerate as you live with your wives, and treat them with respect as the weaker partner and as heirs with you of the gracious gift of life, so that nothing will hinder your prayers. (1 Peter 3:7)

> Husbands, love your wives and do not be harsh with them. (Colossians 3:19)

Just as Ephesians pointed out that Christ loved the church and gave Himself up for her, husbands need to look for ways to sacrifice himself for his mate. I believe that too often we allow self to get in the way of marriage. I recall being told when I got married that marriage was not a fifty-fifty proposition, that each partner was to give one hundred percent in looking after and taking care of their mate, and that selfishness could not be a part of a successful marriage.

That may mean then that as husbands, we might have to give up *Monday Night Football* or maybe a nap or etc. so that we can pay attention to the needs of our mate. Christ leads by unconditional love. Christ does not love us only if we meet His expectations.

Husbands must likewise love their wives in the same manner. So what if you think she's too talkative, too inhibited, or too heavy? We need to love without criticism, comparing, or abusing. I read a story about a trucker who stopped for coffee, and a rough-looking waitress walks up with a tattoo on her arm that says "Charlie." The trucker said, "How's Charlie?" The waitress responded, "Pardon?" "How's Charlie?" the trucker responded. "Oh, that was years ago," she said. "I was high, and it was night, and well, I haven't seen him since. But I'm now married to a wonderful man named Richard. Been married ten years, and he's great." "What does Richard think about Charlie?" "Oh, from the first time I explained it, he has never mentioned it again. I don't think he even sees it anymore."

Christs loves us that very same way, and as husbands, we need to cover and forget our mate's faults in love, the true love of God.

> May your fountain be blessed, and may you rejoice in the wife of your youth. A loving doe, a graceful deer—may her breasts satisfy you always, may you ever be captivated by her love. (Proverbs 5:18–19)

> Enjoy life with your wife, whom you love, all the days of this meaningless life that God has given you under the sun—all your meaningless days… (Ecclesiastes 9:9)

The wives God has given to us are a treasure untold that will always be a blessing, and we need to enjoy the life that God has given to us. I heard it said that if you treat your wife like a thoroughbred, she will seldom act lake a nag. This may sound cute, but as husbands, we must remember that Christ leads by tender kindness, and as our example, we too need to be gentle and considerate with our wives. Men, we need to listen, not just hear, but listen to our wives. Tell her she looks nice, remember anniversaries and birthdays, tell her how special she is, hold her hand, hug her without expectations of a return, let others see publicly that you love her, and respect her as one whom God has provided for you. Christ calls men to leadership because God set up the design, but the leadership is not of power but of love.

Within God's design, what role then does He have for women? In Ezekiel 24:16, a wife is referred to as "the delight of your eyes." We also know that God provided women to be a helper or helpmate to man. When we look at Sarah in the Old Testament, we find Sarah's role with Abraham was one of a Christlike responder. We don't find in the Scriptures that when Abraham said "We'd be moving that," she said "You've got to be kidding." Of course, the Old Testament does not tell us her attitude. It just says she went. We do know that the New Testament talks about attitude.

> Your beauty should not come from outward adornment, such as braided hair and the wearing of gold jewelry and fine clothes. Instead, it should be that of your inner self, the unfading beauty of a gentle and quiet spirit, which is a great worth in God's sight. (1 Peter 3:3–4)

We know how our attitudes reflect upon how we can accomplish things. We also probably realize how our attitudes affect our relationship with our mate.

> Charm is deceptive, and beauty is fleeting; but
> a woman who fears the Lord is to be praised.
> (Proverbs 31:30)

Our attitudes must be wrapped up in Jesus Christ. If He is not the Lord of our life and the one we have a deep reverence for, then our attitudes can get out of control. Our relationship with our husbands can very easily mirror the relationship we have with our God.

> A wife of noble character is her husband's crown, but a disgraceful wife is like a decay in his bones. (Proverbs 12:4)

> A foolish son is his father's ruin, and a quarrelsome wife is like a constant dripping. Houses and wealth are inherited from parents, but a prudent wife is from the Lord. (Proverbs 19:13–14)

The wife that is based in Jesus is a treasure to behold by the husband. He is blessed by the Lord with his wife, and as it mentions in Proverbs 31:28, "Her children arise and call her blessed; her husband also, and he praises her." In order for the wife to be a blessing, she must grow in the Lord, developing the reverent attitude that God desires.

> Wives, submit to your husbands, as is fitting in the Lord. (Colossians 3:18)

> Wives, submit to your husbands as to the Lord. For the husband is the head of the wife as Christ is the head of the church, his body, of which he is the Savior. Now as the church submits to Christ, so also wives should submit to their husbands in everything. (Ephesians 5:22–24)

Just as men don't like the idea of being told they must be sacrificial, women always seem to balk at being told they are supposed to be submissive. But submitting does not mean that you are a doormat. Submitting can mean you have a willingness to share your resources that you have and can give a contribution to your marriage. Submission does not mean being a wimp, but it does mean that we recognize, acknowledge, and respect God's delegated line of authority. When a wife rebels against her husband's leadership, she is rebelling against God's line of authority. That doesn't mean you can't disagree. You can always seek to persuade change. Women can make great changes just by their very behavior through a gentle and quiet spirit.

> Wives, in the same way be submissive to your husbands so that, if any of them do not believe the word, they may be won over <u>without words</u> by the behavior of their wives, when they see the purity and reverence of your lives. (1 Peter 3:1–2, emphasis added)

As I've mentioned, I believe a wife must be a Christlike responder. Philippians 2:5–11 basically says that "your attitude should be the same as that of Christ Jesus: Who…humbled himself and become obedient to death—even death on a cross!" The Bible doesn't say women are subservient to men but that in the family, in the church, man is to be acknowledged as the leader. A compliant, submissive spirit to God's delegated authority is a tribute to your understanding that Jesus is your commander in chief. God's Word (Manufacturer's Handbook) provides many lessons for us to look at for how we are to act, what things we need to do, and what attributes we should carry. We'll touch only on a few, yet you can see many of these throughout the lives of women described in the Old and New Testament.

> In the same way, their wives are to be women worthy of respect, not malicious talkers but temperate and trustworthy in everything. (1 Timothy 3:11)

This passage I like because it points out that wives should be able to acquire the respect of their husbands and of others. It is also noted that there is a tie to what the wife says. The tongue can cause great problems as we know from James, and certainly here I believe it has a significant impact on the wife's respect and trustworthiness.

Notice that this scripture says "trustworthy in everything." This means that as a husband, I can trust my wife with anything I say or leave things in her care. This is an important asset for a wife to have.

> Likewise, teach the older women to be reverent in the way they live, not to be slanderers or addicted to much wine, but to teach what is good. Then they can train the younger women to love their husbands and children, to be self-controlled and pure, to be busy at home, to be kind, and to be subject to their husbands, so that no one will malign the word of God. (Titus 2:3–5)

I know there is a lot that could be said here, but the bottom line is that the older wives who have the maturity need to set the example and to teach what is good. This does not mean that you need to be a formal teacher in a Sunday school class, although it would be great if this could occur. But it does mean that as mature Christian wives, you can take on the responsibility to nurture younger women and to show them how to love their families, what it means to be self-controlled and pure, and what submissiveness to their husbands means. There is a tremendous resource out there that I believe is not being used in the church today that could be a significant benefit to couples today.

In closing, I want to share a story I heard about a husband who had been given a promotion to move to another city. The wife had a top, well-paying position in the city where they were living at the time. When she looked for a position in the new community, all she could find was a much lesser position. They agreed that the promotion for him was good, and both moved with the wife taking the lesser position.

She was asked why she agreed to do this and take a more menial position. Her response was that when she got married, she knew that her husband had to be more important than anything else. She had put her priorities on God and her husband, and it was well worth the price.

We need to remember that God knew what He was doing when He designed marriage. His Word (Manufacturer's Handbook) spells these things out. It is a matter of our being submissive to His delegated authority and putting Christ above all.

RAISIN' UP

We've just finished talking about husbands and wives and the marriage relationship. I believe we need to follow through with the rest of the family. God's plan has set up the core family in the husband and wife in a relationship that should last a lifetime.

God has further put in His Word (Manufacturer's Handbook) information and instruction on family living. The Bible provides many insights for parents and children to grow together as a loving harmonious unit that God would like. As Christians, we need to evaluate our actions and reactions with the Word of God and respond accordingly. As with the marriage relationship, the father has a great responsibility to provide the leadership for the family in their spiritual walk with the Lord. The father is not the dictator but must be the example for the direction you want your family to proceed. This does not mean the mother and children sit back and wait, nor do they say "Well, Dad's not doing such and such, so I don't need to either." As we have discussed in earlier sections, each individual has a responsibility to respond to God. Although the following passage relates to the nation of Israel, I believe that the point is clear for each one of us.

> If you fully obey the Lord your God and carefully follow all his commands I give you today,...All these blessings will come upon you and accompany you if you obey the Lord your God:...Do not turn aside from any of the commands I give you today, to the right or to the left, following other gods and serving them. (Deuteronomy 28:1–14)

Let us begin by looking at parents, Mom and Dad. As parents, we have a responsibility to work together for the good of our children. It is the parents' responsibility to bring children into the world and nurture them in a loving relationship with the focus set upon Jesus. Parents have a unique opportunity from the very beginning to shape the character and thought processes of their children. We need to start from the beginning, sharing the love of Jesus with each child.

> O my people, hear my teaching; listen to the words of my mouth. I will open my mouth in parables, I will utter hidden things, things from of old—what we have heard and known, what our fathers have told us. We will not hide them from their children; we will tell the next generation the praise worthy deeds of the Lord, his power, and the wanders he has done. He decreed statutes for Jacob and established the law in Israel, which he commanded our forefathers to teach their children, so the next generation would know them, *even the children yet to be born*, and they in turn would tell their children. Then they would put their trust in God and would not forget his deeds but would keep his commands. (Psalm 78:1–7, emphasis added)

> Tell it to your children, and let your children tell it to their children and their children to the next generation. (Joel 1:3)

As parents, we fail to be consistent in our teachings with each child and may at times just take it for granted that our children will know. They'll get all this by osmosis. It just isn't so. As parents, we must take the lead and teach.

> The Lord said to Moses, 'Say to the Israelites: "Any Israelite or any alien living in Israel who

> gives any of his children to Molech must be put to death. The people of the community are to stone him. I will set my face against that man and I will cut him off from his people; for by giving his children to Molech, he has defiled my sanctuary and profaned my holy name. If the people of the community close their eyes when that man gives one of his children to Molech and they fail to put him to death, I will set my face against that man and his family and will cut off from their people both him and all who follow him in prostituting themselves to Molech. (Leviticus 20:1–5)

The point to be made here is that many parents, knowingly or unknowingly, have given their children over to the worldly ways. How can this be?

I believe this occurs when as parents, we don't take an active interest in such things as the following:

> What do my children watch on TV?
> What books are my children reading?
> Who are my children's friends?
> Are the activities my child is involved with something I believe is in accord with the Bible?
> Does the clothing my children wear make a statement?
> What kind of games are my children playing?
> What does my child do with the computer?

These are but a few of the things we need to be aware of as they relate to our children. In like manner, we as parents must also review what we also do in these areas as our children learn and respond by example. What kind of example are you?

One area that is hard for parents seems to be discipline. Today discipline seems to be very relaxed and many times does not become discipline for the one being disciplined. We need to look at what God says about discipline and what He suggests and why it is needed.

> And you have forgotten that word of encouragement that addresses you as sons: 'My son, do not make light of the Lord's discipline, and do' not lose heart when he rebukes you, because the Lord disciplines those he loves, and he punishes everyone he accepts as a son.' Endure hardship as discipline; God is treating you as sons. *For what son is not disciplined by his father?*
> If you are not disciplined (and everyone undergoes discipline), then you are illegitimate children and not true sons. Moreover, we have all had human fathers who disciplined us and we respected them for it. How much more should we submit to the Father of our spirits and live! *Our fathers disciplined us for a little while as they thought best*; but God disciplines us for our good, that we may share in his holiness. No discipline seems pleasant at the time, but painful. Later on, however, it produces a harvest of righteousness and peace for those who have been trained by it. (Hebrews 12:5–11, emphasis added)

He who spares the rod hates his son, but he who loves him is careful to discipline him. (Proverbs 13:24)

Discipline your son, for in that there is hope; do not be a willing party to his death. (Proverbs 19:18)

Do not withhold discipline from a child; if you punish him with the rod, he will not die. Punish him with the rod and save his soul from death. (Proverbs 23:13–14)

> The rod of correction imparts wisdom, but
> a child left to himself disgraces his mother.
> (Proverbs 29:15)

The Bible points out that discipline, no matter how distasteful or painful it may seem at the moment, is for the benefit of the one receiving the discipline. However, as parents, we must recognize that no matter how unpleasant it seems at the time, it will "produce a harvest of righteousness and peace for those who have been trained by it." Now I recognize that many today don't believe in the use of the rod. However, we must not look at the rod as a stick or club but as something that will have a profound effect upon the recipient to remember the lesson being taught. I have observed that many parents try a verbal or "stand in the corner" technique on their children and learn years later that something has failed. I can assure you that the same technique does not work with all children, and as parents, we must tailor the discipline to each child and to the reason for the discipline. I also believe that discipline must start at the very earliest of ages. You can't let a child get away with things because they're too young. Children learn at a very early age the difference between right and wrong and how they can con their parents. Parents must be aware of the con jobs and remember what discipline will bring.

> Discipline your son, and he will give you peace;
> he will bring delight to your soul. (Proverbs 29:17)

Fathers have a delicate role here because as the leader of the household he must manage the household well, and should he desire to be a deacon or elder, he must show the qualities of managing his children and household.

> He must manage his own family well and see that his children obey him with proper respect....and must manage his children and his household well. (1 Timothy 3:4–12b)

It is therefore essential for fathers to take the spiritual leadership that God has given them and set the example. Each one must carefully weigh the scriptures as it pertains to your family. Now when it comes to discipline, fathers must be careful that they don't become dictatorial in their attitudes. However, they must command the respect of their children as one who is in authority.

> Fathers, do not *exasperate* your children; instead, bring them up in the *training* and *instruction* of the Lord. (Ephesians 6:4, emphasis added)

> Fathers, do not *embitter* your children, or they will become discouraged. (Colossians 3:21, emphasis added)

I believe that this is where mothers can play a role in helping the father to ensure that the disciplinary actions are appropriate. It is not the time for discussion of what is right or wrong at the time of discipline, but these things should be discussed and thought about before actions are necessary and should be reviewed and adjusted if necessary after any disciplinary actions have been taken.

Dads have a real responsibility to bring their children up in the instruction of the Lord, but they need to look to the leading of the Holy Spirit so as not to discourage their children. Fathers must have compassion on their children as the psalmist points out.

> As a father has compassion on his children, so
> the Lord has compassion on those who fear him;
> (Psalm 103:13)

If as parents we take our responsibilities seriously and raise our children in the ways of the Lord, we can gain great rewards.

> Sons are a heritage from the Lord, children a
> reward from him. (Psalm 127:3)

> Train a child in the way he should go, and when he is old he will not turn from it. (Proverbs 22:6)
>
> The father of a righteous man has great joy; he who has a wise son delights in him. (Proverbs 23:24)
>
> Children's children are a crown to the aged, (Proverbs 17:6a)

Now it's the children's turn to see what the Bible says about them. One of the things that you will see repeated in the Scripture is something you've all heard at home: "Listen to me." Just as parents are trying to get you to listen, not just hear but listen, Jesus is wanting you to give your full and undivided attention to Him that He might give you some wise information that will help you in your life struggles. You can find a lot of this wisdom in Proverbs, but I will give you some excerpts.

> *Listen*, my son, to your father's instruction and do not forsake your mother's teaching. (Proverbs 1:8, emphasis added)
>
> My son, if sinners entice you, do not give in to them. (Proverbs 1:10)
>
> my son, do not go along with them, do not set foot on their paths; (Proverbs 1:15)
>
> My son, if you accept my words and store up my commands within you, turning your ear to wisdom and applying your heart to understanding, and if you call out for insight and cry aloud for understanding; and if you look for it as for silver and search for it as for hidden treasure, then you

will understand the fear of the Lord and find the knowledge of God. (Proverbs 2:1–5)

My son, do not forget my teaching, but keep my commands in your heart, for they will prolong your life many years and bring you prosperity. (Proverbs 3:1–2)

Listen, my sons, to a father's instruction; pay attention and gain understanding. (Proverbs 4:1, emphasis added)

Hold onto instructions, do not let it go; guard it well, for it is your life. (Proverbs 4:13)

My son, pay attention to what I say; *listen* closely to my words. Do not let them out of your sight, keep them within your heart; for they are life to those who find them and health to a man's whole body. (Proverbs 4:20–22, emphasis added)

My son, keep my words and store up my commands within you. Keep my commands and you will live; guard my teachings as the apple of your eye. Bind them on your fingers; write them on the tablet of your heart. Say to wisdom, 'You are my sister,' and call understanding your kinsman; (Proverbs 7:1–4)

Now then, my sons, *listen to me*;...Listen to my instruction and be wise; do not ignore it. (Proverbs 8:32–33, emphasis added)

For whoever finds me finds life and receives favor from the Lord. But whoever fails to find me harms himself; all who hate me love death. (Proverbs 8:35–36)

> The fear of the Lord is the beginning of wisdom, and knowledge of the Holy One is understanding. (Proverbs 9:10)

> *Stop listening* to instruction, my son, and you will stray from the words of knowledge. (Proverbs 19:27, emphasis added)

I believe the Bible (Manufacturer's Handbook) points out very clearly that as children, we must be open and listen to instructions.

We must open our hearts to God and allow Him to work within our lives. We must know that it is through the knowledge of Jesus that we gain understanding, and it is through the opening of our lives to the Holy Spirit that we gain wisdom, starting with our reverence for God and recognizing that He has established the family that we are a part of, and that through this family, we have an ability to grow by adhering to God's direction. This may mean that we will receive discipline which is something that no one likes but is necessary if we are to grow in the way God and our parents want us to grow. Remember Hebrews 12:5–11, which says not to make light of the Lord's discipline and to not lose heart. We are disciplined because we are loved and are accepted as sons and daughters.

> Whoever loves discipline loves knowledge, but he who hates correction is stupid. (Proverbs 12:1)

> Children, obey your parents in the Lord, for this is right. 'Honor your father and mother'—which is the first commandment with a promise—'that it may go well with you and that you may enjoy long life on the earth.' (Ephesians 6:1–3)

> Children, obey your parents in everything, for this pleases the Lord. (Colossians 3:20)

> My son, do not despise the Lord's discipline and do not resent his rebuke, because the Lord disciplines those he loves, as a father the son he delights in. (Proverbs 3:11–12)

Without proper discipline, children can be led astray to the ways of the world and be influenced by others and run amok. It is no parent's desire their children get led away, yet each child has a responsibility as well to look to the Lord.

> Fear the Lord and the king, my son, and do not join with the rebellious, for those two will send sudden destruction upon them, and who knows what calamities they can bring? (Proverbs 24:21–22)

> A wise son brings joy to his father, but a foolish son grief to his mother. (Proverbs 10:1)

> A foolish son brings grief to his father and bitterness to the one who bore him. (Proverbs 17:25)

As part of the family, each child should desire to bring harmony to the household by striving to listen to the ways of the Lord and grow in wisdom.

In closing, we need to remember that as each of us are members of a family and have a responsibility to one another, we should always strive to put God first in our lives. We cannot handle the daily tasks, frustrations, or problems alone, but we can if we center our life upon Jesus, The Word. The Manufacturer's Handbook provides the guidance and knowledge that if we open ourselves to the Holy Spirit, He will lead us to wisdom.

> Trust in the Lord with all your heart and lean not on your own understanding; in all your ways acknowledge him, and he will make your paths straight. (Proverbs 3:5–6, emphasis added)

> Blessed are all who fear the Lord, who walk in his ways. You will eat the fruit of your labor; blessings and prosperity will be yours. Your wife will be like a fruitful vine within your house; your sons will be like olive shoots around your table. Thus is the man blessed who fears the Lord. May the Lord bless you from Zion all the days of your life; may you see the prosperity of Jerusalem, and may you live to see your children's children. (Psalm 128)

> By wisdom a house is built, and through understanding it is established; through knowledge its rooms are filled with rare and beautiful treasures. (Proverbs 24:3–4)

The family is a plan of God to establish the way of the Lord and to spread the Good News that Jesus is Lord of Lords and King of Kings. The family needs to adhere to one another in this turbulent world and be built up in the Lord. For the family to be built up, they must hear the truth constantly and diligently work together in daily devotions. They must recognize how the world's media is sending mixed messages out about the family and make the comparison with the Truth (Bible). Each member of the family must come to love the Lord completely.

> Love the Lord your God with all your heart and with all your soul and with all your mind and with all your strength. (Mark 12:30)

We must love the Lord on every level of our lives in every way. We need to love the Lord emotionally, spiritually, mentally, and physically. Our love must concentrate on the eternal, not on the things that can pass away.

> Do not love the world or anything in the world. If anyone loves the world, the love of the Father

is not in him. For everything in the world—the cravings of sinful man, the lust of his eyes and the boasting of what he has and does—comes not from the Father but from the world. The world and its desires pass away, but the man who does the will of God lives forever. (1 John 2:15-17)

Parents must teach the children consistently, and the ways that the household is operated will set the example and teach the children what the parents think and believe about God. It is, therefore, important that parents give their children Christian education at home and through Bible School. The parents should not just send them to get educated, but parents must set the example by getting educated themselves. This will allow the parents to set a Christian example daily for their children. There is a saying that goes, "A family that prays together stays together."

I like to take it one step further and say that a family that serves the Lord together stays together. Each one must desire to serve the Lord courageously. We can serve the Lord in the work that we do. How we handle ourselves at work displays our love of serving the Lord. Our wealth can certainly be used to serve the Lord if we put it to the task of being used. Our witness, whether by word or deed, is a way to serve the Lord our God, and surely our service can be seen by our words. We need to be prepared to speak of our Savior.

> But in your hearts set apart Christ as Lord. Always be prepared to give an answer to everyone who asks you to give the reason for the hope that you have. But do this with gentleness and respect, (1 Peter 3:15)

> 'Now fear the Lord and serve him with all faithfulness...choose for yourselves this day whom you will serve,... But as for me and my household, we will serve the Lord.' (Joshua 24:14-15)

LEADIN' UP

When we think about leadership, we need to look at it in the context of the Bible (Manufacturer's Handbook). However, before we look at leadership, we must see that a church leader must first and foremost be God's person before he can do his work. Our priorities must be established so that God is first in our lives. We need to have an intimate relationship with Him (example: husband and wife).

Our relationship with God is a growin' affair, and our reliance must be on God, not worldly things (example: Joshua at Jericho in Joshua 6). As Christians, we must realize that Christianity should be our way of life, not a religion. As Moses said in Deuteronomy 32:47, "They are not just idle words for you—they are your life..."

God provides for each of us to grow, mature, and move up in our spiritual relationship with Him. And as our understanding and reliance upon God increases, we gain spiritual authority.

We can't think about leadership without looking at the church and what it is that God has established. The church is described as a body and not an inanimate structure or organization. This is clear from Scriptures when we see that Christ is the head (Ephesians 1:21–22, 4:15–16, 5:22–23) and the church is Christ's body (Ephesians 5:30, Colossians 1:24). Understanding that the church is a body and not an organization helps us to see that the body is made up of many parts (1 Corinthians 12:12–26). Thus all members of the body are interdependent and have equal value and importance. Each member has been given gifts for use in helping the body (1 Corinthians 12:7). Keeping these things in mind, we need to ask ourselves, what is our concept of leadership? Where did this concept come from? Most common thoughts are the CEO approach: one person knows it all, has it all, and controls it all. The second approach is the boss and worker relationship: I'm the boss. You do as I say. I delegate. Where do these ideas come from? In the worldly standard, Satan directs our thoughts away from the Manufacturer's Handbook (Bible) and focuses our attention on the way the world does things. Unfortunately, in many of our congregations today, we see some of these concepts being used. In others, we see a mix of worldly and scriptural approaches. What we must do as God's persons is to recognize that God has provided us with a leadership manual in the Bible (Manufacturer's Handbook). We just need to study it. Jesus called them together and said,

> You know that the rulers of the Gentiles lord it over them, and their high officials exercise authority over them. Not so with you. Instead, whoever wants to become great among you must be your servant, and whoever wants to be first must be your slave—(Matthew 20:25–27)

Too often, men look upon leadership as *positions* of power and authority. They fail to take seriously the fact that all power and authority is Christ's and that leadership is not an office but an opportunity to serve, remaining accountable to the Head of the Body, which is Christ.

As we move on into more depth on leadership, we can ask ourselves many questions, such as the following: What is our approach to leadership in our congregation? Are you willing to serve? What is the basis for leadership? What do leaders do?

In our study on leadership, we need to keep in mind that there are different gifts for different people. However, each gift is given for the express purpose of service to the building up of the body of Christ (Ephesians 4:7, 11–12). We need to start at the beginning, looking at what God has set up in His Manufacturer's Handbook (Bible) as the organizational structure and function of the church. The first point to consider is that the Greek language used in the New Testament is just as exacting in its instruction on organization and function of the church as it is in the matter pertaining to salvation. As Alexander Campbell stated, "Where the Bible speaks, we speak. Where the Bible is silent, we are silent." He also said, "Let us call Bible things by Bible names because if the word is not there, then the idea that the word represents is not there." Therefore, what we find in the New Testament regarding church organization and function of the local congregation is what we must say. Nothing more, nothing less. However, it seems we (the local congregation) don't take this matter as seriously as we do salvation. Why is this? In this day and age, we decide to come up with our own structure, and we interchange terms and names without thought as to the effect. We don't teach the flock what the Bible (Manufacturing Handbook) says in these matters. Our actions rely upon what we have learned from worldly ways and teachings. This seems to indicate that we think to modify God's Word in this way is insignificant, yet when we dilute God's Word with our own, we change the very nature of the leadership for the body that God has provided, and we change the nature of the church. Let's look at God's relationship with the Israelites and the instructions He gave.

> Now if you obey me fully and keep my covenant, then out of all nations you will be my treasured possession… (Exodus 19:5)

> Obey what I command you today. I will drive out before you the Amorites, Canaanites, Hittites, Perizzites, Hivites, and Jebusites. (Exodus 34:11)

> Moses did everything just as the Lord commanded him. (Exodus 40:16, 19, 21, 23, 27, 29, 32)

Noting that Moses responded to God's direction just as God commanded him should make all of God's people realize that we should do likewise and obey what He commands us today.

> It was he who gave (*presented*) some to be apostles, some to be prophets, some to be evangelists, and some to be pastors and teachers, to prepare God's

people for works of service (*ministry*), so that the body of Christ (*church*) may be built up until we all reach unity in the faith and in the knowledge of the Son of God and become mature, attaining to the whole measure of the fullness of Christ. (Ephesians 4:11–13, emphasis added)

Who, therefore, is the minister? Who does the Bible (Manufacturer's Handbook) say does the work of ministering in Ephesians 4:12? Why then do we set aside offices of minister, youth minister, senior minister, etc.? Where have these offices come from in God's leadership manual? Should we not be as exacting in properly identifying leadership and their distinctive roles as we are with immersion versus sprinkling? If the Bible spells it out ("Obey what I command you today" as it says in Exodus 34:11), then we should put it into practice as God has directed if we consider ourselves a New Testament church. We should be able to say that we have done everything *just* as the Lord commanded us. If we elect not to follow scriptural direction because it's not important or it's not the way we want to do it, then we cease to be a New Testament church. If you think names have no meaning, as I have heard some say, then call your wife a harlot, prostitute, cook, dishwasher, etc. instead of your wife.

As we consider leadership, we must look at the basics of leadership, such as ministry. The Greek here refers to the role of caring for and serving people with the idea of trying to get them reconciled to God and stimulate their spiritual growth. As we have seen in Ephesians 4:11–12, the roles of leaders are to "equip the saints for the work of ministry, to build up the body of Christ." Let's look at a couple of examples. In John 5, Jesus said He came to do the work of His Father and what He did mirrored His Father.

> just as the Son of man did not come to be served, but to serve, and to give His life as a ransom for many. (Matthew 20:28)

Now Paul probably lived Jesus' kind of leadership better than anyone.

> Follow my example, as I follow the example of Christ. (1 Corinthians 11:1)

Paul valued truth, not tradition, yet he was steeped in tradition as a Pharisee before he was converted.

> I was advancing in Judaism beyond many Jews of my own age and was extremely zealous for the traditions of my fathers. (Galatians 1:14)

Traditions are hard to walk away from. Traditions exist for tradition's sake. But we can see that Paul made the change. Truth was what he desired, and so should today's leaders. One of the worst things church leaders can do today is accept what has happened in the past as their guide. Even the church's constitution (except the Bible) and by-laws should not control the church. These things must be brought under the guidance and control of God's Word. Paul also denied status for service.

> But whatever was to my profit, I now consider loss for the sake of Christ. (Philippians 3:7)

Paul was willing just to be God's servant. He was willing to step away from being seen as top dog or head honcho.

> For it seems to me that God has put us apostles on display at the end of the procession, like men condemned to die in the arena. We have been made a spectacle to the whole universe, to angels as well as to men. We are fools for Christ, but you are so wise in Christ! We are weak, but you are strong! You are honored, we are dishonored! To this very hour we go hungry and thirsty, we

are in rags, we are brutally treated, we are homeless. We work hard with our own hands. When we are cursed, we bless; when we are persecuted, we endure it; when we are slandered, we answer kindly. Up to this moment we have become the scum of the earth, the refuse of the world. (1 Corinthians 4:9–13)

We must be careful not to set up little groups (cliques) that are more committed to human or worldly ways than to Christ's lifestyle.

Many times, it becomes too easy for the leadership to look at themselves as superior to the rest of the body.

We also see that Paul did not demand his rights.

> Though I am free and belong to no man, I make myself a *slave* to everyone, to win as many as possible. (1 Corinthians 9:19, emphasis added)

> To the weak I became weak, to win the weak. I have become all things to all men so that by all possible means I might save some. (1 Corinthians 9:22)

Paul used the spirit of encouragement, love, and trust to motivate people to do their best for Jesus. He was given authority to build people up, not to tear them down. Likewise, church leaders must persuade their flock to be obedient by encouragement, love, and motivation. The authority described in the Bible for elders is not found in their role but in their message and their Lord. Paul is seen in most instances as working with people and not over them. His leadership was guiding lovingly through service. Paul considered every member of God's family important. For him, there is never a nobody in Christ's church, as is pointed out in 1 Corinthians 12:12–31. There is not inferiority versus superiority, for this weakens the church, the body of Christ. We also see that he trusted people with responsibility (1 Timothy 1:3, Titus 1: 5).

He sent Timothy and Titus with significant responsibilities rather than taking the attitude of "I'll do it myself" or "They don't do it the way I would." Again, we see Paul was flexible and could relate to people without compromise, and he was a peacemaker. He didn't criticize or chew out people, but he talked and prayed with them. Paul did not use secular approaches to leadership. He didn't look to worldly standards, such as finding ways to succeed, but instead recognized that we must take captive every thought (idea) to make it obedient to Christ.

> I beg you that when I come I may not have to be as bold as I expect toward some people who think that we live by the standards of this world. For though we live in the world, we do not wage war as the world does. The weapons we fight with are not the weapons of the world.
> On the contrary, they have divine power to demolish strongholds. We demolish arguments and every pretension that sets itself up against the knowledge of God, and we take captive every thought to make it obedient to Christ. And we will be ready to punish every act of disobedience, *once your obedience is complete.* (2 Corinthians 10:2–6, emphasis added)

Keeping all of the above information in mind, we can see from a cursory review of the New Testament that leadership is essential for the church to grow. Godly leadership is extremely important for the health of the congregation. This type of leadership, servant leaders under the authority and Lordship of Christ, helps the body to flourish. Let's begin looking at leaders as established in the Bible (Manufacturer's Handbook) by recognizing that we need to look at these leaders in terms of the work, not the office. By looking at the leadership roles in terms of work rather than the office position, we can focus on the good work God has designed for these men to do.

Elders, shepherds, pastors, and overseers are terms that the Bible uses for the men who are to teach, pray for, and care for the spiritual needs of the congregation. They also govern and lead the church as servants who set the example and provide the model for Christian life. If these men shift their perception of eldership away from that of a position and toward the work, then they can understand what their role is as pointed out in Acts 20.

> Keep watch over yourselves and all the flock of which the Holy Spirit has made you overseers. Be shepherds of the church of God, which he bought with his own blood. (Acts 20:28)

This is the good work of the elders. One has to pay attention, be concerned about, and care for the flock to ensure the flock is protected from the worldly influences. A shepherd feeds, protects, and cares for those that God has given him to look after.

Elders are Christians whom the Holy Spirit has matured into leaders for the body. They are not going to be perfect or flawless, but looking at all the qualifications in the Bible, it appears they should be blameless. This does not mean they are sinless, but their moral conduct is above reproach inside or outside the body of Christ.

> Here is a trustworthy saying: If anyone sets his heart (*desires*) on being an overseer, he desires a noble task (*good work*). Now the overseer must be above reproach, the husband of but one wife, temperate, self-controlled, respectable, hospitable, able to teach, not given to drunkenness, not violent but gentle, not quarrelsome, not a lover of money.
>
> He must manage his own family well and see that his children obey him with proper respect. (If anyone does not know how to manage his own family, how can he take care of God's church?) He must not be a recent convert, or he

may become conceited and fall under the same judgement as the devil. He must also have a good reputation with outsiders, so that he will not fall into disgrace and into the devil's trap. (1 Timothy 3:1–7, emphasis added)

First, we see that for one to be an elder or overseer, he must set his heart on or desires to be, because he lusts after the good work. The Greek for *desire* can also be translated as "lusts after." One wants very much to do the work that God has laid out for this role.

A person who desires to be an elder wants to guard and protect the flock, feed the lambs the Word of God so they mature, be an example, and equip the flock for works of service or ministry.

An elder must be a man of integrity. He must be above reproach, respectable, blameless (free from the accusations of evil). He must be the husband of but one wife (the Greek literally says "a one-woman man"). An elder expresses his marital faithfulness and sexual purity by living in fidelity to his marriage covenant. One must be temperate. An elder must be able to control his temper and not let his emotions rule his judgement. An elder must also be self-controlled in his actions related to alcohol, money, and the pastoral authority he uses in the church. He can't have the attitude so often displayed in the world of "my way or the highway." He must be respectable, meaning his life exhibits spiritual discipline and a commitment to a holy lifestyle, loving what is good. An elder must be a lover of strangers (hospitable).

He is willing to provide help to all who need help or service and is not so preoccupied with his own situations that he cannot find time to help others. An elder must be able to teach and defend the faith. He must have a solid biblical foundation and personal convictions to train the flock in the great truths of the faith and to have the courage to confront people when they are wrong. Then we see a list of nots that a man desirous of the role of elder needs not to be involved in through his life. Not addicted to wine indicates he must not be controlled by alcoholic influence. One must not want to resort to fighting, quarreling, or physical actions to deal with situations. A man interested in the eldership is not fond of sordid gain and has no involvement with dishonest money matters or greediness. He does not believe he has to compromise the rules in order to make a profit. An elder must manage his own family well. Since leading a church body is similar to handling a family, the elder must be a man who loves, cares, and leads his family well. He must lead his family in such a manner that his children are faithful and obedient to the father's leadership. An elder must not be a recent convert. This means an elder must be spiritually mature, someone who knows Jesus, has been around in Christ's body and the Word, and has been in fellowship with God's people. He must be very familiar with the heart and mind of God so that he does what God wants him to do. An elder's reputation must be good among those outside the church.

Outsiders should not see him as a person who acts holier than thou, nor one who has loose morals. Outsiders should have genuine respect for his integrity and character.

Let's take some time to look at the work of the eldership. In an overview of the New Testament, we can see that the elders are shepherds of God's flock and have a responsibility to lead, feed, protect, and care for God's people.

> Keep watch over yourselves and all the flock of which the Holy Spirit has made you overseers. Be shepherds of the church of God, which He bought with his own blood. (Acts 20:28)

Elders must continually examine themselves and be interested in the spiritual growth of the whole flock. They must have the concern of the flock as top priority.

> To the elders among you, I appeal as a fellow elder, a witness of Christ's sufferings and one who also will share in the glory to be revealed. Be shepherds of God's flock that is under your care, serving as overseers—not because you must, but because you are willing, as God wants you to

be; not greedy for money, but eager to serve; not lording it over those entrusted to you, but being examples to the flock. (1 Peter 5:1–3)

As overseers for God's flock, elders are to serve willingly. They are desirous of caring for the flock without being concerned with "What's in it for me?" Their leadership is by example so God's people can see what they should do and how they should act instead of leading with power and authority. Elders have a responsibility to feed the church, and one of the best ways to feed is for the elders to provide a positive influence through teaching.

> Now I commit you *to God and to the word of his grace*, which can build you up and give you an inheritance among all those who are sanctified. (Acts 20:32, emphasis added)

Teaching is one of the ways good elders can lead the flock by turning the lights on or showing the church the way. Elders have a responsibility to equip the saints for the work of service or ministry.

> It was he who gave some to be apostles, some to be prophets, some to be evangelists, and some to be pastors and teachers to prepare *God's people for work of service*, so that the body of Christ may be built up... (Ephesians 4:11–12, emphasis added)

In addition, there are other references in the New Testament regarding elders work:

1. Praying over the sick (James 5:14)
2. Dispensing of benevolence for saints (Acts 11:30)
3. Diligently leading and caring for God's flock (Romans 12:8)

Caring for God's people is the very core of an elder's work. An elder who is dedicated to serving God will be a good shepherd that is committed to his flock. He will develop loving relationships with the people, and the flock will recognize that he is someone they depend on when needed.

Let's look at another role in the body of Christ. In the New Testament, there are two words for servant in the Greek. After a review of the words, it seems that in 1 Timothy 3, the word is used to describe those that are in charge of a special service or function. The Greek for this word has also been translated as servant and minister. Carefully looking at the usage of these words, we see two things that stand out. One, we see generic roles as servants, and we see special roles as minister or deacon. Therefore, it appears that deacons are special servants who have spiritual maturity and spiritual qualities.

We find in 1 Timothy 3:8–12 qualifications for deacons, and these can be viewed in the same sense as qualifications for elders.

> Deacons, likewise are to be men worthy of respect, sincere, not indulging in much wine, and not pursuing dishonest gain. They must keep hold of the deep truths of the faith with a clear conscience. They must first be tested; and then if there is nothing against them, let them serve as deacons. In the same way, their wives are to be women worthy of respect, not malicious talkers but temperate and trustworthy in everything. A deacon must be a husband of but one wife and must manage his children and his household well. (1 Timothy 3:8–12)

The next work of leadership service that we will look at is the role of the evangelist. What specifically is the work of an evangelist? Romans 1:15 points out that Paul was eager to preach the gospel.

> But you, keep your head in all situations, endure hardships, *do the work of an evangelist*, discharge all the duties of your ministry. (2 Timothy 4:5, emphasis added)

In this day and age, we have changed the terminology of the New Testament and call the evangelist the preacher or minister, yet the words of the New Testament refer to the evangelist as the one proclaimer of God's Word. He proclaims God's Word not only through the sermons and teachings he does before the body but also proclaims God's Word through his living message. The evangelist shares and assists the elders in the role of bringing the body into the fullness of Christ. In 2 Timothy, we see many directives given to the evangelist to follow.

> Keep reminding them of these things. Warn them before God against quarreling about words; it is no value, and only ruins those who listen. Do your best to present yourself to God as one approved, a workman who does not need to be ashamed and who correctly handles the word of truth. Avoid godless chatter, because those who indulge in it will become more and more ungodly. (2 Timothy 2:14–15)

The evangelist must hold fast to the teachings of scripture, carefully reading and studying what is revealed. He is in charge, along with the elders, to "prepare God's people for works of service" (Ephesians 4: 11–12). He is to make disciples of Jesus, grounding them in God's Word, modeling the Christian life among them, bringing them toward maturity, and training to reproduce. In summary, the evangelist has the role to proclaim God's Word, teaching people the genuine doctrine of God's Word and assisting God's people to live with the teachings of the Word in the world.

The leadership of a local body should have a goal of having a healthy congregation. For this to occur, the leadership must work together as a team to ensure the following:

1. The people have a sense of security in their relationships together.
2. The people have meaningful, healthy communication patterns.

3. The people have meaningful interactions beyond the scheduled worship times.
4. The people have a clear sense of their purpose and the direction they are headed.
5. The leadership has a clear vision and a clear sense of where the body is in the process of attaining that vision.

The main and necessary ingredient for the leaders to have a healthy congregation is prayer. They need to pray together regularly. Their prayers need to be directed for the flock, for each other, and for the lost.

Prayer will help the leaders to bond together with God in directing the mission of the church. Prayer will help the leadership to recognize that they are to lead the flock under the direction of the head, Jesus Christ, and not by themselves. Prayer will also help the leadership remember that the church has a mission for reaching the lost and that they are responsible for leading the flock in fulfilling that mission.

> His intent was that now, through the church, the manifold wisdom of God should be made known to the rulers and authorities in the heavenly realms, according to his eternal purpose which he accomplished in Christ Jesus our Lord. (Ephesians 3:10–11)

> And he made known to us the mystery of his will according to his good pleasure, which he purposed in Christ, to be put into effect when the times will have reached their fulfilment-to bring all things in heaven and on earth together under one head, even Christ. (Ephesians 1:9–10)

> And pray for us, too, that God may open a door for our message, so that we may proclaim the mystery of Christ. (Colossians 4:3)

MATURIN' UP

We have covered areas of moving up individually, by couples, and by family through leadership, so we now come to the moving up or maturing as the body of Christ, The Church. Jesus prayed that we may all be brought to complete unity to let the world know that God sent Him as written in John 17.

> My prayer is not for them alone, I pray also for those who will believe in me through their message, that all of them may be one, Father, just as you are in me and I am in you. May they also be in us so that the world may believe that you have sent me. I have given them the glory that you gave me, that they may be one as we are one: I in them and you in me. *May they be brought to complete unity to let the world know that you sent me* and have loved them even as you have loved me. (John 17:20–23, emphasis added)

As previously mentioned, the church is the body of Christ (Ephesians 1:22). We see in Colossians 1:17–20 that Christ is the head of the body, The Church, so that He has supremacy over everything. As the head, we find that Jesus wants the church to work together in unity. He also set the organization up with the people who should prepare all members of the body for works of service so the body may be built up until all reach unity in the faith and knowledge of the Son of God and become mature.

> Make every effort to keep the *unity of the Spirit* through the bond of peace. There is *one body and*

> *one Spirit*—just as you were called to one hope when you were called—<u>*one Lord, one faith, one baptism, one God and Father of all,*</u> who is over all and through all and in all. (Ephesians 4:3–6, emphasis added)
>
> It was he who gave some to be apostles, some to be prophets, some to be evangelists, and some to be pastors and teachers, to prepare God's people for works of service, so that the *body of Christ may be built UP until we all reach unity in faith and in the knowledge of the Son of God and become mature,* attaining to the whole measure of the fullness of Christ… Instead, speaking the truth in love, we will in all things grow up into him who is the Head, that is Christ. (Ephesians 4:11–13, 15, emphasis added)

If God has designed the Church with Christ as the head, why do we have so many different bodies expressing so many different ideas about knowing Christ and obtaining salvation? Paul talks about divisions in the church in 1 Corinthians 1:10–17, and it should remind us of who we really follow, Christ or the men, who established our particular group of bodies. It appears to me that we have been accepting things that have been passed down through the ages without fully verifying them with the Bible. As one man said to me, if it was good enough for my parents and grandparents, it is good enough for me.

> I appeal to you, brothers, in the name of our Lord Jesus Christ, that all of you *agree with one another so that there may be no divisions among you and that you may be perfectly united in mind and thought.* My brothers, some from Chloe's household have informed me that there are quarrels among you. What I mean is this: One of you says, "I follow Paul"; another, "I follow Apollos";

> another, "I follow Cephas", still another, "I follow Christ".
>
> Is Christ divided? Was Paul crucified for you? Were you baptized into the name of Paul?... For Christ did not send me to baptize, but to preach the gospel—not with words of human wisdom, lest the cross of Christ be emptied of its power. (1 Corinthians 1:10–17, emphasis added)

A number of years ago, a young fellow asked how to determine where to attend church. He said, "There are so many different churches. How do you know who is right?" My comment to him was to study the scriptures and compare the scriptures with what the various bodies practiced. Then you attend the body that practices what the Bible teaches.

Why then do we have so much division in the churches today? It appears to me that so much of what is occurring is due to the world's influence. Culture has become dominant over what the Bible presents. As mentioned in the chapter on growin' up, we need to determine who or what occupies first place in our lives. It seems apparent that so much of our activities is centered on pride. If we change what we believe, then we are admitting that we were wrong. But why should we care if we went down the wrong track if we realize that we now know the truth because the Bible tells us so?

> We who are strong ought to bear with the failings of the weak and not to please ourselves. Each of us should please his neighbor for his good, to build him up. For even Christ did not please himself but, as it is written: "The insults of those who insult you have fallen on me." For everything that was written in the past was written to teach us, so that through endurance and the encouragement of the scriptures we might have hope. May the God who gives endurance and encouragement give you a *spirit of unity* among yourselves as you

> follow Christ Jesus, so that with *one heart and mouth* you may glorify the God and Father of our Lord Jesus Christ. Accept one another, then, just as Christ accepted you, in order to bring praise to God. (Romans 15:1–7, emphasis added)

It seems that rather than following the directions the Manufacturer's Handbook (Bible) provides for a church organization, many bodies have taken the worldly approach. It seems clear to me that the Bible provides a simplified organization of elders, deacons, and evangelists all at the local level, where many bodies have established headquarters over several bodies and the headquarters direct what the local bodies do. Looking at the Bible (Manufacturer's Handbook) for proper direction, we see that the Head of the Church, be it local or worldwide, is Christ. What other headquarters do we need? For Christ, as Head of the Church, has been given all supremacy. "For God was pleased to have all his fullness dwell in him" (Colossians 1:19). If we then believe this, we should recognize that the Church should follow the directions that God has provided in the Bible, just as we as individuals should recognize and follow all the directions and authority presented to us.

> So then, just as you received Christ Jesus as Lord, continue to live in him, rooted and built up in him, strengthened in faith as you were taught, and overflowing with thankfulness. See to it that no one takes you captive through hollow and deceptive philosophy, which *depends on human tradition and the basic principles of this world* rather than Christ. (Colossians 2:6–8, emphasis added)

> Since you died with Christ to the basic principles of this world, why, as though you still belonged to it do you submit to its rules. (Colossians 2:20)

Why then do we continue to provide our directions in worldly approaches instead of adhering to the principles and directions of the Bible? Oh, I know. Many have told me that what I shared with them was just my interpretation, but they interpret it differently. However, we must realize that the interpretation should only come from the Holy Spirit and that man's ideas don't carry any weight.

> Above all, you must understand that no prophecy of scripture came about by the prophet's own interpretation. For prophecy never had its origin in the will of man, but men spoke from God as they were carried along by the Holy Spirit. (2 Peter 1:20–21)

Paul addressed some of these matters in his letters and in reference to those letters we find Peter referring to them.

> He writes the same way in all his letters, speaking in them of these matters. His letters contain some things that are hard to understand, which ignorant and unstable people distort, as they do the other scriptures, to their own destruction. Therefore, dear friends, since you already know this, be on your guard so that you may not be carried away by the error of lawless men and fall from your secure position. (2 Peter 3:16–17)

We can also find that Paul encouraged all to press on to the goal that God has provided. If we are truly wanting to grow in Christ and reach the prize that calls us, then we need to work at learning what God provides and what Jesus wants with the Church—unity. If we believe in the Holy Spirit being here to lead us into all truths, then let us consider this.

> Not that I have already obtained all this, or have already been made perfect, but I press on to take

> hold of that for which Christ Jesus took hold of me. Brothers, I do not consider myself yet to have taken hold of it. But on one thing I do: *Forgetting what is behind and straining toward what is ahead.* I press on toward the goal to win the prize for which God had called me heavenward in Christ Jesus. All of us who are mature should take such a view of things. *And if on some point you think differently, that too God will make clear to you.* (Philippians 3:12–15, emphasis added)

It appears to me that we need to forget what is behind and move forward with Christ's Church maturing as it should with unity. Where there are differences we who are mature need to stand up and look to God to help us see what is right in His sight, not ours.

As members of the body of Christ, we have the responsibility to teach sound doctrine and teach so that all may be equipped for good works.

> You must teach what is in accord with sound doctrine. (Titus 2:1)

> All scripture is God-breathed and is useful for teaching, rebuking, correcting, and training in righteousness, so that the man of God maybe thoroughly equipped for every good work. (2 Timothy 3:16–17)

It is time that the body of Christ moves toward maturity by using THE WORD as the standard for Christ's Church. We need to "conduct yourselves in a manner worthy of the gospel of Christ" (Philippians 1: 27), doing what is right in accordance with the Manufacturer's Handbook (Bible). As it states in Philippians 2:14, we need to "Do everything without complaining or arguing," so that we can focus on what the scriptures are saying regarding the Church. Our goal should be to see that the body of Christ is doing what God has shown us through His Word. He desires unity for the bride of Christ and not division. It should be incumbent upon us as his followers to strive to obtain that unity by adhering to the Bible.

> And let us consider how we may spur one another on toward love and good deeds.
> Let us not give up meeting together, as some are in the habit of doing, but let us encourage one another—and all the more as you see the Day approaching. (Hebrews 10:24–25)

Therefore, let us all strive to be a part of helping as Christ moves us in bringing unity to the Bride, the body of Christ. The key for us is to allow the Holy Spirit to work in us and direct our thoughts and actions. We need to rely wholly upon the Holy Spirit and not put out the Spirit's fire (1 Thessalonians 5:19), for God wants us to move forward in maturing so that the Church, the body of Christ, matures in unity to let the light of Jesus impact the world. We need to let the world know that there is only one Church, Christ's Church, the body of Christ. And by showing this unity, the world will come to know that salvation comes only through Jesus Christ our Lord.

> May the God of peace, who through the blood of the eternal covenant brought back from the dead our Lord Jesus, that great shepherd of the sheep, *equip you with everything good for doing his will, and may he work in us what is pleasing to him*, through Jesus Christ, to whom be the glory forever and ever. Amen. (Hebrews 13:20–21, emphasis added)

SUMMARY

We could continue to explore what the Bible (Manufacturer's Handbook) has to say about moving up as individuals, church leaders, or even as a church body. However, I hope we are able to see that moving up in the Lord is a matter of commitment that each one must make with our Lord to show that you want to serve Him and Him alone. Once we've made the commitment, then we can actively engage Christ in our thinking, our speaking, and our activities. We must start by giving GOD FIRST PRIORITY.

Notice I said FIRST PRIORITY. No, hunting does not come before God. No, sports do not come before God. No, _____ do not come before God. Moving up with the Lord is similar to moving up in your position at work, progressing along in school, or moving along in whatever activities you want. Moving up takes commitment, work, dedication, desire, stick-to-itiveness, etc. You achieve the goals of your desire because you reach for it. Likewise, if you desire to achieve the goal of moving up in the likeness of Jesus Christ, you must also reach out and reach up, and God will be there to assist you in your determination to be more Christlike, whether as a leader or as an individual member of Christ's body.

> Not that I have already obtained all this, or have already been made perfect, but I press on to take hold of that for which Christ Jesus took hold of me. Brothers, I do not consider myself yet to have taken hold of it. But one thing I do: Forgetting what is behind and straining toward what is ahead. I press on toward the goal to win

the prize for which God has called me heavenward in Christ Jesus. (Philippians 3:12–14)

We have much to say about this, but it is hard to explain because you are slow to learn. In fact, though by this time you ought to be teachers, you need someone to teach you the elementary truths of God's word all over again. You need milk, not solid food! Anyone who lives on milk being still an infant, is not acquainted with the teaching about righteousness. But solid food is for the mature, who by constant use have trained themselves to distinguish good from evil. Therefore, let us leave the elementary teachings about Christ and go on to maturity... And God permitting, we will do so. (Hebrews 5:11–6:3)

We want each of you to show this same diligence to the very end, in order to make your hope sure. We do not want you to become lazy, but to imitate those who through faith and patience inherit what has been promised. (Hebrews 6:11–12)

ABOUT THE AUTHOR

Robert Kaiser, better known as Bob, grew up in Robinson, Illinois, and went to a denominational church. Although he had an interest in the Bible and wanted to live according to God's Word, he graduated from Colorado School of Mines with a degree in petroleum engineering. His interest in the scriptures continued, and after much study, he was immersed into the death, burial, and resurrection of Jesus. Empowered by the Holy Spirit, he became involved with planting several New Testament churches. He has been preaching the gospel for over forty-five years through interim ministries. During the past twenty-five years, he has given seminars on Christian growth, marriage, and families. In addition, he established an RV ministry of service known as Servants of Our Savior. Bob's aim has always been to help Christians mature in their relationship with God.